MAGICAL
FAIR

FANTASY CREATURES

Gareth Stevens PUBLISHING

HOT TOPICS

BY BENJAMIN PROUDFIT

Please visit our website, www.garethstevens.com. For a free color catalog of all our high-quality books, call toll free 1-800-542-2595 or fax 1-877-542-2596.

Library of Congress Cataloging-in-Publication Data
Names: Proudfit, Benjamin.
Title: Magical fairies / Benjamin Proudfit.
Description: Buffalo, NY : Gareth Stevens Publishing, 2026. | Series: Fantasy creatures | Includes glossary and index.
Identifiers: ISBN 9781482475302 (pbk.) | ISBN 9781482475319 (library bound) | ISBN 9781482475326 (ebook)
Subjects: LCSH: Fairies–Juvenile literature.
Classification: LCC GR549.P93 2026 | DDC 133.43–dc23

Published in 2026 by
Gareth Stevens Publishing
2544 Clinton Street
Buffalo, NY 14224

Designer: Leslie Taylor
Editor: Kristen Nelson

Photo credits: Cover (fairy), 5 (evil fairy), 9, 15, 17 Shutterstock AI Generator/Shutterstock.com; cover and series art (neon circle) Ikrill/Shutterstock.com, (rough frame) TarnishArt/Shutterstock.com, (splotchy background) TiffanyShanks/Shutterstock.com; p. 5 (sweet fairies) krisArt/Shutterstock.com; p. 11 Christies_Angelica Kauffmann/_File:Angelica Kauffmann - Calypso calling heaven and earth to witness her sincere affection to Ulysses.jpg_commons.wikimedia.org; p. 13 Excavations of Paul-Émile Botta, 1843]1844/_File:Blessing genie Dur Sharrukin.jpg/_commons.wikimedia.org; p. 18 Olga Popova/Shutterstock.com; p. 19 Presented by the Trustees of the Feeney Charitable Fund, 1925/File:Sandys, Frederick - Morgan le Fay.JPG_commons.wikimedia.org; p. 21 John Simmons/File:John Simmons - Titania sleeping in the moonlight protected by her fairies.jpg_commons.wikimedia.org; p. 23 Allstar Picture Library Ltd/Alamy.com; p. 25 (both photos) Elsie Wright/File:Cottingley Fairies 1.jpg and File:CottingleyFairies3.jpg_commons.wikimedia.org; p. 27 Hethers/Shutterstock.com; p. 29 (fairy door) Dwight Burdette/File:Fairy door at Peaceable Kingom Ann Arbor Michigan.JPG_commons.wikimedia.org, (fairy garden) Jenn Huls/Shutterstock.com; p. 30 (gnome) Susie_p_art/Shutterstock.com, (leprechaun) Christos Georghiou/Shutterstock.com.

Printed in China

CPSIA compliance information: Batch #QWGS26: For further information contact Gareth Stevens, at 1-800-542-2595.

CONTENTS

Many Fairies

Maybe you think of a fairy as a tiny, humanlike being with wings and a bit of magic. You may have read a **fantasy** story with an evil fairy—but they were the size of a person! Fairies, and creatures like them, have been shown in many ways throughout history.

IMAGINE THAT!

THE WORD "FAIRY" COMES FROM AN OLD FRENCH WORD.

Some fantasy books use "faerie" or "fae" when talking about fairies. In many cases, changing the spelling doesn't mean anything. But, in some stories, this change in spelling shows the magical beings are wicked or more powerful.

IMAGINE THAT!

PIXIE AND SPRITE ARE NAMES USED FOR TWO KINDS OF FAIRIES.

Fairy Features

Fairies are commonly beautiful beings. Stories often say they live longer than humans do. In some tales, fairies can see what is to come. They mostly live in their own land, apart from humans. But fairies and humans sometimes fall in love in stories!

IMAGINE THAT!

A FAIRY RING IS A RING FOUND ON THE GROUND, OFTEN IN GRASS, THAT IS A DIFFERENT COLOR THAN THE GROUND AROUND IT. STORIES SAY THE RING IS CAUSED BY FAIRIES DANCING!

In the Past

Fairy-like beings are found in **mythology**. Greek myths tell of nymphs. These were female spirits connected to nature. For example, dryads were nymphs found in forests and trees. Calypso is a nymph in the Greek story the *Odyssey*. She offers the hero Odysseus immortality.

IMAGINE THAT!

IMMORTALITY MEANS BEING UNABLE TO DIE. MANY FANTASY STORIES SAY FAIRIES ARE IMMORTAL.

Other **cultures'** mythology have fairy-like creatures too. Jinni (or jinn) are spirits found in Arabic myths. These creatures have powers and use them unseen by humans. They are said to be able to look like a person or animal. Jinni may harm humans that harm them.

IMAGINE THAT!

JINN, SOMETIMES SPELLED DJINN, HAVE BECOME PART OF SOME MUSLIMS' BELIEFS.

JINNI

Irish Fairies

Irish myths say a magical group called the Tuatha de Danann were some of the first people to live in Ireland. After being **defeated** by other early Irish people, the Tuatha de Danann went underground. They became Sidhe—fairies!

IMAGINE THAT!

IN SOME IRISH STORIES, FAIRIES LIVE IN THE OTHERWORLD. IF A HUMAN HAS A SPECIAL WAY OF SEEING, THEY CAN FIND THEIR WAY THERE THROUGH CAVES, TREES, AND OTHER NATURAL PLACES.

In Irish stories, fairies and humans often meet. Humans try to keep fairies away by wearing necklaces made of certain woods or flowers such as marigolds. That's because fairies might steal a person away. They might make the human work for fairies for seven years!

IMAGINE THAT!

TIME IN THE FAIRY WORLD HAS BEEN SAID TO WORK DIFFERENTLY THAN HERE. IF A PERSON WAS STOLEN FOR SEVEN YEARS, MORE OR LESS TIME MAY HAVE PASSED IN THE HUMAN WORLD.

Through the Middle Ages

Many fairy stories can be traced back to the **Middle Ages**. It was during this time that the word "fairy" began to be used. The stories of King Arthur included a fairy named Morgan le Fay that could heal people. Even her name sounds like a fairy!

MORGAN LE FAY

IMAGINE THAT!

MORGAN LE FAY IS ALSO THE NAME OF A COMIC BOOK CHARACTER! SHE WAS INTRODUCED IN 1955 IN THE COMIC *BLACK KNIGHT*.

Shakespearean Fairies

Writer William Shakespeare created his plays in the late 1500s and early 1600s. *A Midsummer Night's Dream* features the king of fairies, Oberon, and the queen of fairies, Titania. Shakespeare's works show fairies that are more like **nobles** and less like fairies of old folktales.

IMAGINE THAT!

PUCK, ANOTHER FAIRY IN *A MIDSUMMER NIGHT'S DREAM*, PLAYS TRICKS ON OTHERS.

TITANIA

Peter Pan and Tinker Bell

Since the 1950s, many people have **created** their idea of fairies from the **animated** movie *Peter Pan*. It features a tiny, lovely female fairy named Tinker Bell. Peter Pan and Tinker Bell were first introduced in the play *Peter Pan*, written in the early 1900s.

IMAGINE THAT!

DISNEY MADE THE ANIMATED *PETER PAN* MOVIE, AMONG OTHER MOVIES AND SHOWS FEATURING TINKER BELL. DISNEY HAS MADE MANY MOVIES BASED ON FAIRY TALES. BUT NOT ALL FAIRY TALES HAVE FAIRIES IN THEM!

Cottingley Fairies

In 1917, two girls took photos of something amazing—fairies! Not everyone thought they were real pictures. But a well-known writer, Arthur Conan Doyle, saw the photos in 1920 and believed. His interest helped them get the photos **published** in a magazine.

IMAGINE THAT!

IN THE EARLY 1980S, THE GIRLS FINALLY TOLD THEIR STORY. THE FAIRY PHOTOS WERE FAKE! THEY USED HATPINS TO HANG UP FAIRIES ONE OF THEM DREW AND CUT OUT.

COTTINGLEY FAIRIES PHOTOS

Fairies Today

Fairies are featured in many fantasy books and movies today. The *Artemis Fowl* book series brings readers into the fairy world as a boy tries to save his family. The show *Winx Club* is about a girl who finds out she is a fairy and goes to a school to learn more.

IMAGINE THAT!

THE POKÉMON CARD GAME INTRODUCED FAIRY-TYPE POKÉMON IN 2013. CLEFAIRY, TOGEPI, AND SYLVEON ARE ALL FAIRY-TYPE.

Have you ever left your tooth under your pillow for the tooth fairy? Or set up a fairy garden with a little house or tiny furniture? These practices show that many people still enjoy fairy stories today—and maybe even believe!

IMAGINE THAT!

IN ANN ARBOR, MICHIGAN, THERE ARE FAIRY DOORS FOUND ON THE FRONT OF SOME BUILDINGS THROUGHOUT THE DOWNTOWN AREA.

FAIRY DOOR IN ANN ARBOR

FAIRY GARDEN

A Lot Like Fairies

HERE ARE A FEW OTHER FANTASY CREATURES THAT ARE A BIT LIKE FAIRIES.

BROWNIE

in Scottish folktales, a spirit that lives in houses and comes out at night to help out

DWARF

in folktales, a small humanlike being that is often very skilled at making things

ELF

in fantasy stories, a magical being that looks like a tall, beautiful human, but they live a very long time

KOBOLD

in German stories, a kind of trouble-making spirit

GNOME

a dwarf that keeps some kinds of treasure safe

LEPRECHAUN

in Irish folktales, an elf that may cause trouble and knows where treasure is

FOR MORE INFORMATION

BOOKS

Munsey, Lizzie, et al. *Supernatural Creatures: Mythical and Sacred Creatures from Around the World.* New York, NY: DK, 2024.

Nardo, Don. *Creatures and Beasts in World Mythology.* San Diego, CA: ReferencePoint Press, Inc., 2025.

WEBSITES

Fantasy Books for Kids
https://www.commonsensemedia.org/lists/fantasy-books-for-kids
Find lots of great fantasy books for kids here.

Fantasy Movies for Kids
https://www.commonsensemedia.org/lists/best-fantasy-movies
Find your next favorite fantasy movie here!

GLOSSARY

animated: Consisting of drawings or computer images that appear to move.

create: To bring into being.

culture: The beliefs and ways of life of a group of people.

defeat: To beat.

fantasy: Having to do with imaginative stories that feature impossible events and characters.

Middle Ages: A time in European history from about 500 to 1500.

mythology: The stories told by a people to explain practices, beliefs, or natural events.

noble: Someone born into the upper classes.

publish: To put out in a newspaper, book, or magazine.

INDEX